The Countries
Afghanistan

Bob Italia
ABDO Publishing Company

visit us at
www.abdopub.com

Published by ABDO Publishing Company, 4940 Viking Drive, Edina, Minnesota 55435. Copyright © 2002 by Abdo Consulting Group, Inc. International copyrights reserved in all countries. No part of this book may be reproduced in any form without written permission from the publisher.

Printed in the United States.

Photo Credits: Corbis
Art Direction & Maps: Neil Klinepier

Library of Congress Cataloging-in-Publication Data

Italia, Bob, 1955-
    Afghanistan / Bob Italia.
        p. cm. -- (The countries)
    Includes index.
    Summary: Examines the history, geography, people, government, economy, and art and recreation of Afghanistan.
    ISBN 1-57765-653-9
    1. Afghanistan--Juvenile literature. [1. Afghanistan.] I. Title. II. Series.

DS351.5 .I86 2002
958.1--dc21

                                                2001053818

Contents

Hello from Afghanistan!

Hello from Afghanistan. The country has had a long and troubled history. Long ago, ancient empires and other invaders conquered the region. In modern times, foreign countries and Afghan tribes have fought for control of its scorching deserts, fertile valleys, rolling plains, and snow-capped mountains. Afghanistan's harsh land makes it difficult for plants and animals to flourish.

Afghanistan has about 20 **ethnic** groups. They have their own tribes, language, and **culture**. Almost all Afghans are Muslims. Most Afghans work in agriculture.

Afghanistan's major political groups share power in government. Kabul is the capital and largest city of Afghanistan.

It is difficult to travel in Afghanistan. Years of war have damaged many roads. But the country has a national airline. And it has a national radio station and television station.

Religion dominates Afghanistan's holiday seasons. Religious holidays are celebrated according to the **Islamic** calendar.

Folklore, folk songs, and folk dances play an important part in Afghan life. They help Afghans pass on their values and traditions from one generation to the next.

Hello from Afghanistan!

Fast Facts

KABUL

OFFICIAL NAME: Republic of Afghanistan
CAPITAL: Kabul

LAND
- Highest Peak: Nowshak 24,557 ft. (7,485 m)
- Major River: Helmand

PEOPLE
- Official Languages: Pashto and Dari
- Population: 24,977,000 (2002 est.)
- Major Cities: Kabul, Kandahar
- Religion: Islam

GOVERNMENT
- Form: Factional government
- Head: Chairman
- National Anthem: "Sorode Meli" ("National Anthem")

ECONOMY
- Agricultural Products: Barley, corn, cotton, fruits, sheepskins, mutton, nuts, rice, vegetables, wheat, wool
- Manufactured Products: Cement, processed foods, rugs, shoes, textiles
- Mining Products: Coal, lapis lazuli, natural gas
- Money: Afghani (100 pule = 1 afghani)

Afghanistan's flag

Bundled Afghanis

Timeline

100,000 B.C.	Prehistoric hunting people live in Afghanistan
4000 to 2000 B.C.	First cities appear
1500 B.C.	Aryans invade
mid-500s B.C.	Persians invade northern Afghanistan
A.D. 600s	Arab Muslim armies sweep into Afghanistan
900 to 1200	Turkish peoples rule Afghanistan
1200s	Genghis Khan and the Mongols conquer Afghanistan
1500s to 1700s	Safavids and Mughals struggle for control
1747	Afghan tribes unite for the first time
1819	Civil war breaks out
1826	Dost Mohammad Khan gains control
1800s	Britain and Russia compete for control of Afghanistan
1880	'Abdor Rahman Khan becomes emir
1919	Emir Habibullah Khan is assassinated; Afghanistan becomes fully independent
1929	Mohammad Nader Shah becomes king
1931	Afghanistan adopts a new constitution
1933	Nader Shah assassinated; Mohammad Zahir Shah becomes king
1964	Afghanistan adopts a new constitution
1973	Zahir Shah overthrown; Mohammad Daud Khan becomes president
1978	Military leaders revolt; Daud Khan is killed
1979	Soviet Union invades Afghanistan
1988	Soviet Union withdraws from Afghanistan
late 1990s	The Taliban takes control of government
2001	Taliban is forced from power

A Troubled History

Alexander the Great

About 100,000 years ago, **prehistoric** people lived in what is now Afghanistan. Around 1500 B.C., the Aryans came to Afghanistan. The Persians conquered northern Afghanistan in the mid-500s B.C.

About 330 B.C., Alexander the Great conquered Afghanistan. In about 246 B.C., the Afghans revolted and took control of their land.

In the A.D. 400s, the Kushans took Afghanistan. Soon after, the Sasanians and the Huns defeated the Kushans.

Arab Muslims came to Afghanistan during the late 600s. Between 900 and 1200, many Arabic peoples ruled Afghanistan. In the 1200s, Genghis Khan and the Mongols conquered Afghanistan.

After the Mongol empire crumbled, many different peoples ruled Afghanistan. In 1747, Afghan tribes were united under the leadership of Ahmad Shah Durrani.

In 1819, a civil war began. It ended in 1826 when Dost Mohammad Khan gained control and became the **emir**.

In the 1800s, Great Britain wanted to protect its empire in India from Russian invasion. So it decided to take control of Afghanistan. Britain's 1839 invasion of Afghanistan started the First Anglo-Afghan War, which ended in 1842. In 1878, another British invasion started the Second Anglo-Afghan War.

In 1880, 'Abdor Rahman Khan became emir. He gave the British control of Afghanistan's foreign relations. Rahman Khan worked to create a strong national government. After he died in 1901, his son, Habibollah Khan, took over.

In 1919, Habibollah Khan was **assassinated**. One of his sons, Amanollah Khan, became **emir**. His troops attacked the British and started the Third Anglo-Afghan War. Afghanistan gained its independence that year.

Amanollah Khan

Amanollah Khan wanted to modernize Afghanistan. Its first **constitution** was adopted in 1923. In 1926, Amanollah Khan became king. But tribal and religious leaders did not like the changes. They forced Amanollah from power in 1929.

In 1929, Mohammad Nader Shah became king. Two years later, Afghanistan had a new constitution. But Nader Shah was assassinated in 1933. His son, Mohammad Zahir Shah, became king.

In 1953, Mohammad Daud Khan, the king's cousin, made himself **prime minister**. But Daud Khan had difficulties, and resigned in 1963.

In 1964, under Zahir Shah's leadership, Afghanistan adopted yet another **constitution** that provided for a **democratic** government. But democracy failed with Afghanistan's tribal system.

In 1973, Daud Khan overthrew Zahir Shah and established the **Republic** of Afghanistan. Daud Khan became president.

Mohammad Nader Shah

In 1978, rival Afghans supported by the Soviet Union revolted, and Daud Khan was killed. This group took control and formed a **Communist** government. Many Afghans, called *mujahideen* (holy warriors), opposed the new government and its policies, which went against **Islamic** teachings. They began attacking government forces.

In 1979, the Soviet Union invaded Afghanistan to help fight the rebels. The Soviets had superior weapons. So the rebels fought a **guerrilla** war to overcome this advantage.

In 1989, the Soviet Union withdrew from Afghanistan. The *mujahideen* and government forces continued fighting until 1992.

Afghanistan had several *mujahideen* governments after 1992. But fighting continued among different political groups.

In the late 1990s, a group known as the Taliban took control of most of Afghanistan. The Taliban believed in strictly following **Islamic** law. Many freedoms, especially for women, were restricted or forbidden. The Taliban severely punished those who broke the law.

In 2001, the United States accused the Taliban of helping the **terrorists** who attacked New York City and Washington, D.C., on September 11. The United States demanded that the Taliban arrest the terrorists.

The Taliban refused. After relentless U.S. bombing and attacks by Afghan opposition forces, the Taliban was driven from power in December 2001.

Afghan schoolgirls wearing the traditional burqa veil. Under Taliban rule, women who showed their faces in public were punished.

All four of Afghanistan's major political groups shared power in a newly formed government. But it was unclear if the new government could hold together as Afghans began the difficult task of rebuilding their war-torn country.

Smoke and dust rise after a U.S. airstrike on Taliban forces.

An Afghan man holds up a picture of Afghanistan's former king, Mohammad Zahir Shah, as Afghans celebrate the liberation of their city by Afghan opposition forces.

The Land

Afghanistan has three main land regions. They are the Northern Plains, the Central Highlands, and the Southwestern Lowlands.

The Northern Plains have **plateaus** and rolling hills. The Central Highlands cover much of Afghanistan. The snow-capped Hindu Kush mountain range is here, including Nowshak at 24,557 ft. (7,485 m), its highest peak. Most Afghans live in the Hindu Kush's high, narrow valleys.

The Southwestern Lowlands have desert or semidesert lands. Here, the Helmand River flows from the Hindu Kush to the Sistan Basin on the Iranian border. The basin has salty lakes and marshes.

North America
Europe
Asia
Africa
South America
Australia
Antarctica
DETAIL AREA

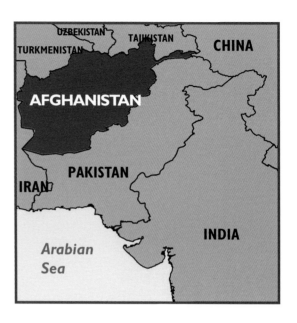

UZBEKISTAN
TAJIKISTAN
TURKMENISTAN
CHINA
AFGHANISTAN
IRAN
PAKISTAN
INDIA
Arabian Sea

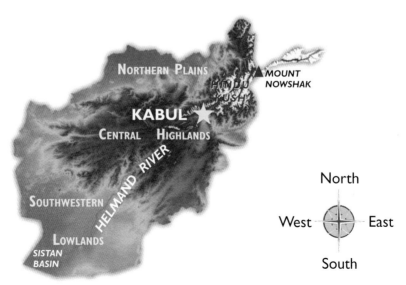

NORTHERN PLAINS
MOUNT NOWSHAK
HINDU KUSH
KABUL
CENTRAL HIGHLANDS
HELMAND RIVER
SOUTHWESTERN
LOWLANDS
SISTAN BASIN

North
West — East
South

Overall, Afghanistan is a **semi-arid** country with hot summers and cold winters. Temperatures are warmest in the Northern Plains and the Southwestern Lowlands, where it is also the driest. The Central Highlands is the coolest region, and it receives the most rainfall.

Travelers on a highway near Hindu Kush

Rain

Rainfall

**AVERAGE YEARLY
RAINFALL**

Inches		*Centimeters*
Under 10		*Under 25*
10 - 20		*25 - 50*
20 - 59		*50 - 150*

Temperature

**AVERAGE
TEMPERATURE**

Fahrenheit		*Celsius*
Over 68°		*Over 20°*
50° - 68°		*10° - 20°*
32° - 50°		*0° - 10°*
14° - 32°		*-10° - 0°*

North

West ⊕ East

South

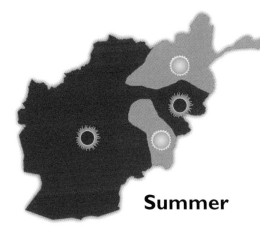

Summer

Winter

Plants & Animals

Afghanistan's harsh land makes it difficult for plants and animals to flourish. Most plants are found in the north. Large forests of pine and fir trees grow in the mountainous regions. Cedar, oak, walnut, alder, ash, and juniper trees are found at the lower altitudes. There are also shrubs, roses, honeysuckle, hawthorn, and currant and gooseberry bushes.

There is not much vegetation in southern Afghanistan. But in the rainy season, the deserts are covered with flowering grasses and herbs.

Few large animals live in Afghanistan. The Siberian tiger has almost disappeared. Wolves, foxes, striped hyenas, jackals, gazelles, wild dogs, and snow leopards live in the mountains and foothills. Wild goats and sheep are in the mountains. Brown bears can be found in the mountains and forests. There are also mongooses, moles, shrews, hedgehogs, bats, and kangaroo rats.

Afghanistan's bird population includes pheasant, quail, cranes, pelicans, snipes, partridge, crows, vultures, and eagles. Many kinds of fish live in Afghanistan's rivers, streams, and lakes. The rivers on the northern slopes of the Hindu Kush are known for their brown trout.

The Siberian tiger has almost disappeared from Afghanistan.

The Afghans

A Pashtun elder

Most Afghans are **descendants** of peoples who invaded or settled the land. These groups include Aryans, Persians, Arabs, Turks, Mongolians, and Chinese.

Afghanistan has about 20 **ethnic** groups. They have their own tribes, language, and **culture**.

The largest ethnic groups are the Pashtuns and the Tajiks. Most Pashtuns live in the southeast. They speak Pashto, one of Afghanistan's two official languages.

Afghanistan's **nomads** are mostly Pashtun herdsmen. They live in goat-hair tents and transport their belongings on the backs of camels, donkeys, and cattle.

Most Tajiks live in central and northeastern Afghanistan. Tajiks and many other groups speak Dari, the other official language. Most are farmers and craftspeople.

Most Afghans wear traditional clothing. A heavy **felt** or sheepskin coat is common in the winter. Rural men wear a turban that often identifies their tribal group. City women wear a *chadri*, a full-length hooded garment. Rural women cover their heads with a shawl.

Afghans serve flat loaves of bread at every meal. Vegetables, yogurt, chicken, beef, **mutton**, and rice are also popular. Fruits and nuts are common dessert items. And tea is the favorite drink.

Almost all Afghans are Muslims. Religion plays an important part in everyday life. Almost every Afghan village or group has a religious leader, called a *mullah*. They help explain **Islamic** law and teach the children.

Law requires all Afghan children from 7 to 15 years old to go to school. But many children cannot attend because of a lack of schools or teachers. Afghanistan has two universities, Ningrahar University in Jalalabad and Kabul University.

Afghan children read at a school in a mosque. The five-year-old sister of a mujahideen *fighter is the class's only girl.*

Rice Pudding (Sher Berinj)

1/4 pounds of rice
1 pint of milk
4 oz. sugar

4 oz. sultanas
Rose water or vanilla
Pistachio nuts

Wash the rice and spread it out on a flat board to dry. When completely dry, crush to a third of the size of the grain. Boil the milk and allow it to thicken, stirring constantly. When it is reduced to three-quarters of the original quantity, add the rice and cook for a few minutes. Add sugar and sultanas, and cook until you have a thick custard (10 to 15 minutes). Remove from heat and flavor to taste with rose water or vanilla. Sprinkle with pistachio nuts. Serve hot or cold. Serves four.

AN IMPORTANT NOTE TO THE CHEF: Always have an adult help with the preparation and cooking of food. Never use kitchen utensils or appliances without adult permission and supervision.

LANGUAGE

English	Pashto
Afghanistan	Afghaanistaan
American	Amrikaayi
Canada	Kaanaaddaa
Father	Plaar
Grandfather	Baabaa
Grandmother	Anaa
Uncle	Akaa

Where They Live

Kabul and Kandahar are two of Afghanistan's major cities. Kabul is Afghanistan's capital and largest city. It is the center of **economic** and **cultural** activity. The city **exports** carpets, sheepskins, and fruits and nuts. Its industries make medicines, farm tools, furniture, machine tools, plastics, **prefabricated** houses, **textiles**, and wine.

Kandahar is Afghanistan's second-largest city. It is part of an important trade route that links India, Iran, Pakistan, and Kabul. It also processes and exports fruits. Kandahar's older part has many ancient buildings and **bazaars**. The city also has modern areas.

Afghanistan's city dwellers live in homes and apartment buildings made of baked brick or concrete, or both. Farmers usually live in small villages in river valleys. These villages are often built like small forts, containing several mud houses and closely connected families.

Afghan homes

Economy

Most Afghans work in agriculture. Wheat is the main crop. Afghans also grow barley, corn, cotton, fruits, nuts, rice, sugar beets, and vegetables.

Livestock is also an important agricultural product. The **semi-nomadic** people raise most of the country's livestock. The main livestock products are dairy items, **mutton**, wool, animal **hides**, and sheepskins.

Afghanistan is rich in minerals, including natural gas, coal, copper, gold, and salt. The country also has large deposits of iron ore, but much of it has not been mined.

Afghanistan leads the world in the production of the precious stone lapis lazuli. Other valuable stones include amethysts and rubies.

A few Afghan mills produce **textiles**. Small factories make cement, matches, and processed foods. Craftworkers make gold and silver jewelry, leather goods, and rugs.

A family winnowing grain

A New Government

The Taliban was forced from power in 2001. Afterward, all four of Afghanistan's major political groups shared power in a newly formed government. The groups were supporters of the former king; a group of **exiles** based in Cyprus, Greece; another group based in Peshawar, Pakistan; and the Northern Alliance military leaders who successfully fought the Taliban for control of Afghanistan.

The four Afghan groups signed an agreement on December 5, 2001. Hamid Karzai, a Pashtun tribal commander, acted as chairman of the new government. Tribal delegates also chose a 29-member **administration**.

As chairman, Karzai had five vice chairpersons. The new government also had 23 ministers and deputy ministers.

The new **administration** also brought back a role for women in public life. It allowed women education and employment once again, and included them in government. At least one of the five vice chairpersons and one of the 23 ministers were female. The new government also made plans for a national army and supreme court.

Hamid Karzai

The new government would rule for six months. At the end of six months, a national assembly of Afghan tribal leaders, or a *loya jirga*, would meet to approve another government. This government would then remain in power for two to three years while a **constitution** was drafted. Elections would be held at the end of this period to elect leaders of a permanent government.

Transportation & Communication

Afghanistan has about 11,700 miles (18,800 km) of roads. Most paved roads were damaged during the Soviet invasion. Afghanistan's most famous transportation route is the Khyber Pass. It has been an important trade route for centuries. The country has no railroads. But it does have an international airport

A Television of Afghanistan news broadcast by two unveiled Afghan anchorwomen shortly after the fall of the Taliban government

in Kabul. Afghanistan's national airline is Ariana Afghan Airlines.

Afghanistan has five newspapers. The country has one national radio station and one national television station, called Television of Afghanistan.

Several men walk alongside a donkey caravan on Khyber Pass at the Pakistan-Afghanistan border.

Religious Holidays

Religion dominates Afghanistan's holiday seasons. Religious holidays are celebrated according to the **Islamic** calendar.

Eid-al-fitr marks the end of the holy month of Ramadan. New clothes are worn to prayer services. Afterward, people visit friends and families. Children usually receive gifts or money, called *eidi*.

Eid-al-adha is celebrated on the tenth day of the 12th month of the Islamic calendar. The day honors the prophet Abraham's willingness to sacrifice his son. People visit friends and families, and exchange gifts.

Mawleed al-nabi is celebrated on the 12th day of the month Rabi al-Awal in the Islamic calendar. On this day, people celebrate the prophet Muhammad's birthday.

They attend prayers, remember Muhammad, and visit friends and family.

Jeshen is on August 19. It marks Afghan independence from British control of its foreign policy.

Nowroze falls on March 21. It celebrates the first day of spring.

Afghans dance in celebration of the start of the holy Muslim fasting month of Ramadan in Herat, a city in western Afghanistan.

Arts & Recreation

Folklore, folk songs, and folk dances play an important part in Afghan life. They help Afghans pass on their values and traditions from one generation to the next.

One folk dance is a Pashtun war dance called the *attan*. It re-enacts the **martial** life of the Pashtuns' ancestors. It is the national dance of Afghanistan.

Afghans enjoy rugged sports and games. Many men like to hunt. Some use Afghan hounds as hunting dogs. Men of the Northern Plains play a game called *buzkashi*. Dozens of horsemen try to grab a headless calf and carry it across a goal.

Afghan horsemen play the traditional game of **buzkashi.**

Index